The Aging Poems

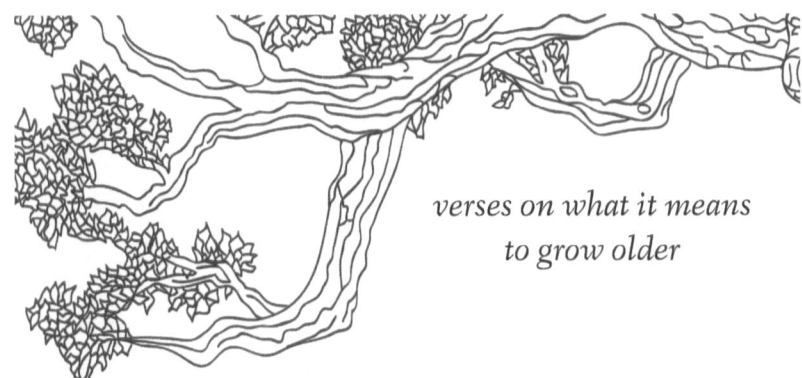

*verses on what it means
to grow older*

The Grand Avenue Poetry Collective

Sylvia Cavanaugh, Nancy Harrison Durdin, Dawn Hogue,
Maryann Hurtt, Georgia Ressmeyer, Lisa Vihos,
and Marilyn Zelke Windau

WATER'S EDGE PRESS
Sheboygan, Wisconsin | Tucson, Arizona

Copyright © 2018 by Water's Edge Press

All rights reserved. This book or any portion thereof
may not be reproduced or used in any manner whatsoever
without the express written permission of the publisher
except for the use of brief quotations in a book review.

Printed in the United States of America

ISBN-978-0-9992194-2-3
ISBN: 978-1-952526-15-2

Library of Congress Control Number: 2018955862

Water's Edge Press LLC
Sheboygan, WI | Tucson, AZ

watersedgepress.com

This is a work of imagination. Names, characters, businesses, places, events
and incidents are either the products of the authors' imagination or used in
a fictitious manner. Any resemblance to actual persons, living or dead, or
actual events, is purely coincidental.

The typeface used in this book is Fanwood

Book design by Dawn Hogue
Images from Getty Images

Also by The Grand Avenue Poetry Collective:

The Water Poems

Contents

Sylvia Cavanaugh

Seed Pod	3
Stitched Reflection	4
Hot Flash	5
Waiting Room	6
Oak in Spring	7

Nancy Harrison Durdin

Separate Lives in Little Packages	11
Letting Go and Moving On	12
Tick Tock	13
Maybe Morning is Enough	14
The Timekeeper	15

Dawn Hogue

Out, Damned Sock	19
The Easter Lily	20
Fatigue	22
Barn Quilt	23

Maryann Hurtt

Crane Mountain, Every Mountain	27
Tai Chi at the Senior Center	28
The Long Toll	29
Ragtag Rodeo Clown Dance	30
After How Many Years	31

Georgia Ressmeyer

Not Soon, Not Yet	35
Her Eyes	36
Mind Leaving	37
That Sinking Feeling	38
Not Giving Up	39

Lisa Vihos

Looking for Joy	43
Fall and Spring	44
Vanitas	45
In the Infancy of My Old Age	46
Reversal	47

Marilyn Zelke Windau

Gotcha	51
Ache Age	52
Perennial	53
To Heal or Not Too Heel	54
Threads	55

Sylvia Cavanaugh

Seed Pod

Phantasmagoric play of vermillion
violet, indigo, russet
lemon and flame
all a sizzle in summer's sunshine
hands clasped in joyous expectation
wind breathes down her spine
and she sways into dance

this was before she saw the leaves
scuttle across the sidewalk
the brown gleam of horse chestnuts
collected in her hand
she skipped alongside the butterscotch
laughter of her aunt
thinking of school paste
and carefully cut construction paper

and wondering how music can be written
as notes on lines
measured in bars
when all these things happen...
the summer, the sizzle
the arrangement of color
clasp of hands
all of it
all at once
in the memory of her waning years
music like lift-off
like wind
flying

Stitched Reflection

The Fates measured life in lengths
of string. I sewed a sampler quilt-top
one winter when I was twenty. I cut

each thin scrap and angled them
flat with my thin steel needle. Fifty
years later, I'm finally getting around

to the quilting. Two layers embrace
the batting as my needle weaves in
and out, parallel to each seam in the

pattern. I double-cross the broken dish
and shoo-fly a coffin star. Spin through
the whirlwind of positive pregnancy

tests. I tease out the devil's puzzle of
a drunken man's logic. A bird's nest
of excuses gives way to providence

and a hidden star. As I inch across this
textile mirror, my needle gently pricks
the finger hidden behind the honeycomb.

Hot Flash

To forge weapons
with fire
is a sign that we are civilized
but the taste of knowledge
had its price
dealt in a currency
of fertility
in calendar clicks of counted days
a real blood bargain
paid periodically
paid in labor pains and
in pre-menstrual syndromes

but now I wield
my own damned fire
to cauterize the wound
the first sin settled up
my womb
now sweated caustic clean
Adam's bones are mine
and he is scorched
turning on these embers
he re-arranges and adjusts
looks at me
across his stiff
cold shoulder
and winks

Waiting Room

A room waits for the end of my life. Most
of us finish this way, confined to a single
room for weeks, months, sometimes years.

Women especially know this truth and it
creeps into conversation. The waiting room,
biding its time. The skilled men and women

who built my waiting room may have thought
about its future occupants. Or, my room may
not have even been built yet, or the builders

not yet born. I'll keep to myself in my room.
My three children will be too busy or live
too far away. These days I carry my room

past great oaks, into opera, and the youthful
exuberance of my classroom. I carried it as
a child when I roamed back alleys and river

valleys. I want to greet this room as a friend.
I will examine the corners and fill each one
with my thoughts. A hospital room started

my life's journey. A whole week's nursery
stay in 1960. Shocked by newfound hunger
and terrible light, I couldn't see the corners.

Oak in Spring

Shadowy roots secure themselves
and finger into blackened loam
they whisper of a private grace

while the stolid sentry
stands its ground
naked and dark above the earth
rooted down to March

she shoulders the burden
of watchful eyes
and of a secret knowing
that living skin
could feel like stone
and sweat
an emerald bloom

Nancy Harrison Durdin

Separate Lives in Little Packages

Years separated into little packages of life,
strung along on a very long timeline.
The earlier ones get harder to imagine
having been in; seeing myself as that
person gets harder to believe.
Luckily, there are old photographs
to prove I was in those lives.

The long parade of loved ones,
so essential and important to me,
unthinkable at the time to not
have them with me; yet
I do not have them now,
and still my life goes on.

Some live on in memory only,
some have gone on to other lives:
missed, but slowly replaced by others,
now so important in my life.
I go on adding and discarding pieces
of me, learning from what I have been,
to better understand who I am now.

I look forward to, and anticipate
the changes that await me,
as I add more little packages of time
to this long, long, line of mine.

Letting Go and Moving On

Rising at the end of the day
from my seat of accountability
for the last time.

I let my familiar white coat slide
off my shoulders until it lay
in puddles of relief at my feet.

The cool fresh wind of change
hit me in the face,
catching my breath,
turning me around
toward a door marked
"Forever More."

I stepped into my future
through that door.
I thought I heard the
sound of clapping as
I walked away.
I did, it was me!

Tick Tock

Old Man Time will have his way so they say,
but what about Old Woman?

Will she have her day
when time has licked
the wounds clean
as she's fading into gray?

Will Old Man Time allow her
a slow dance
with a youthful lover,
a graceful exit,
her dreams fulfilled?

Or will he demand and pout,
use his clout,
have her leave in silence,
a song still in her head...
lips parted
ready to sing?

Maybe Morning is Enough

    Inspired by Billy Collins' poem, "Morning" Picnic, Lightning, 1998

Why don't we stop with morning?
The sun opening our eyes
is all the proof we need that
we have lived through another night
and have a brand new day ahead.

A quick glance around the room
tells us we are where we are
supposed to be at this moment,
books and magazines still in place,
slippers waiting for our feet,
right where we left them.

He gets up first, I stay
in bed for awhile now because
I can if I want to, most days.
I look out the window, at the
soaring tree tops and the birds.

Soon, the smell of coffee wafts in
the air, and a distant radio plays,
letting me know that he loves me
enough to make coffee, even
though, he drinks tea.

Maybe we should stop with morning;
is it going to get better than this?

The Timekeeper

I walk in a new direction, forward.
The wind at my back
like the palm of a hand
pushing me forward,
always forward.
The timekeeper walks behind me
with his swinging lantern,
sometimes I glance over
my shoulder as he looks
at his timepiece, and smiles.

Dawn Hogue

Out, Damned Sock

I wanted to hit this dirty sock. To be precise,
it's clean now, folded with its mate, subdued
and submissive. But before it got itself thrust
into the washer, I wanted to sock it in the mouth,
the damn thing. Twice it escaped the bundle of clothes
I had enveloped in my arms to cart downstairs.
It must have thought it could get away. Maybe
it even smirked as it lay at the bottom of the steps,
wriggled and ready to dart before I grabbed it
and crammed it back into the over spilling
heap of darks in my arms.

I wanted to hit 60, too, but it pummeled me
into acceptance, and now 62 has me against the ropes.
This defeat has made it all the harder to bounce back
when sneaky little socks leap out of laundry bundles
piled so high in my arms that I fail to see another bundle,
this one in a basket my thoughtful husband has brought down
and placed logically in the doorway of the laundry room.
Because I am unaware, I move with manic energy and trip,
diving forward, my arms outstretched as if to steal second,
my momentum over the dirty clothes below me
a perfect crescendo. I land with a thwomp so hard
it resounds throughout the house.

Resting, babying my wounds, I feel foolish.
In my younger days, I possessed such a keen sense
of self-awareness that I often marveled at how others
could not foresee those single moments that lie ahead, ready
to thwart. I suppose, now and then, I looked on them and smirked.
More than once I probably thought: How did you not see that coming?
Don't think this irony is lost on me. It is a bitter acknowledgement
that age has won, this small battle at least. So instead of raising a fist,
I lie down for a nap and accept that I am not now that strength
which in old days moved earth and heaven—
that which I am, I am.

But still, I blame the damn sock.

The Easter Lily

    For Eunice, my neighbor

It's nearly November and your Easter lily
has bloomed. White as a sun-filled cloud,
white as an eagle feather, white as sharp light.

And I thought you would be pleased to know it.

I remember you, stooped shouldered,
leaning on your cane, supervising your son,
who at your direction unearthed the florist-shop lily
from its gold-cellophane-wrapped pot, its petals
long fallen, its green-tongued leaves still strong.
You pointed to the spot near the climbing rose
where you wished it to go, and dutiful,
as always, he dug the hole.

92 you were then.

I recall our conversation
one afternoon later that spring.
You had come out on your back porch
for air and sun. You sat upon the top step
with such fatigue I wondered
how you had managed at all.
"I won't be here much longer," you said,
and I, as I expected I should reply,
countered you, but I now think
doing so was a demeaning gesture,
both to honesty and to your desire
to see your life fulfilled.

Five years later, late July,
long after you hoped you would,
you died. Life's rhythms you kept
until you could not, your son driving you
in your last years to Mass each Saturday night,
Friday morning hair appointments,
the grocery store each week. You did it all
until the four steps of your back porch
became a mountain.

But that day from my kitchen window
I saw him tamp the earth for you
and sprinkle the soil, and when he stood
and brushed the dirt from his hands,
you seemed satisfied that he had given in
to your whim to keep the prospect of
perennial blooms, even if they might
be blooms you would never see.

You would be surprised to know it bloomed
after a good frost, though it must have felt
protected there under the canopy of rose leaves
curtseying their last goodbyes.

The week before your funeral, your son
held you by the arm as a gentleman escort,
and led you slowly into your back yard,
where like a tiny shadow you stood, your head
and neck fighting against the buttress of your
curved spine to look up, to view the wild bed
you and I both loved. Each year an endless show:
daffodil white, tulip red, poppy orange,
yarrow yellow, phlox pink.

You must have known.

The wild bed is asleep now.
They say we will have a mild winter.
The tenacious lily seems to suggest so.
And it purely gleams.

Fatigue

I stretch my length upon my bed
and feel suddenly that I am now
the tiny and hollow-boned carcass
of my life at ninety, having born
the weight of all my sine waves,
highs and lows, joys and sorrows,
yesterdays and tomorrows.

Elastic, I will return to myself
come morning, but tonight,
in December's bold dark,
the end of all has shown itself to me.

I will pass in that time,
giving up not just the
weight of my body
but everything
that meant
or mattered.

In that moment,
I will move for the last time,
sense for the last time,
beat for the last time,
exhale for the last time,
and become infinitely
small in eternity,
a frequency only
intermittently audible
beyond me.

Barn Quilt

Inspired by the art quilt, Barn With No Bats by Kathleen Erbek

The deep purple evening star
fades on Aunt Gracie's barn
and spent raspberry canes wither,
ready to be cut down for mulch.
Soon the stone walk will disappear
as will the still vigorous grass
she hasn't the time to mow
under downy blankets of snow
that only birds
or her snowshoes will disturb.
It is an autumn sky,
the morning haze lifted
to a light yellow afternoon.
In the fruit cellar, she rustles
through yesterday's bushel for us,
finding the best unblemished apples.
Seven bushels line the wall,
the best for pies, the others to press,
the fallen she leaves for bees,
or if she's lucky one evening, a doe.
Later, in our own home,
we speak of her, we say
perhaps this is her last year,
that she's getting so frail,
unaware that in her bones
a young girl awakens
with each step up the ladder,
each glint of russet catching her eye.

Maryann Hurtt

Crane Mountain, Every Mountain

some days you just take
one step
then the next
up and over and through
ladders, boulders, stick out roots
believe in tendons, bone
ligaments
know your heart
keeps pumping
blood
where it's supposed to go
you climb higher
trust
some invisible faith
till all that sweat
baptizes your almost doubting
self
and you get up
take another step
breathe deep
and begin again

Tai Chi at the Senior Center

we slip through the motions
wave hands like clouds
repulse the monkey
balance on one leg just
for that moment
before we find gravity
either friend
or foe
but these times
of grace when it's possible
to laugh
even as we teeter
understand down deep
our bodies
were made for just this
sacred foolishness
the way the wrinkles-crinkles
around our eyes
are tiny wren tracks
our snowy hair
another way
to say
we have lived
vertical now, horizontal
whenever
but right now
simply and most abundantly
alive

The Long Toll

maybe the trick
to what we all desire
is to simply crawl in
late at night
hear breaths in and breaths out
sleep the kind
of sleep
where you nest
next to someone you love
even more
the grayer we become
learning love
may be bells and whistles
but the long toll
is what gives rhythm
rhyme and reason
to all our days

Ragtag Rodeo Clown Dance

maybe it really isn't too late
to be the rodeo clown
I always dreamed
here I am sixty
and I better start right now
'cause you never know
when bulls come barreling
out of the chutes
ready to carry you
to some kingdom come
and I better learn to flirt
head on
with crazed animals
than never entering the arena
so let me do my ragtag
rodeo clown
save my sorry dusty butt
dance
and let me do it
one gracious step
at a time

After How Many Years

not just silence
but the kind of quiet
where you hear
cottonwood roots
sink deeper and deeper
and at last
find the kind of water
that eases a thirst
you thought
could never be found

Georgia Ressmeyer

Not Soon, Not Yet

Restless autumn will not stand
and wait. It will fly off the branch
as bird or leaf, will rustle
to the wind's erratic lurch,
amplify its stay on earth.

I, too, will crunch and crackle,
sway, escape the limb,
not let the snow already feathering
my head become a goose-down quilt
to tuck me in.

With flocks of leaves I will go
skipping through the town,
see the sights, scrape the ground,
not fall softly into winter's nest.
Not soon. Not yet.

Her Eyes

Today her eyes rebel against seeing.
She defers to their wishes, doesn't clean
her glasses or force herself to squint
at distant objects.

"Free yourself from depending on us,"
her eyes advise. "Experience the world
with your hands, ears, toes, the tip of your
nose. Remember how it felt to be a toddler."

She decides focus won't matter, traffic
patterns, memorizing new people's features.
Nothing will capture her keenest visual
attention. She'll boycott straining to see.

Her eyes will not be "corrected" to any
conventional standard. They insist
on staying quirky, unpredictable, strangely
defective, refusing to get up early.

She doesn't argue with her eyes, which
may not zoom but do allow her, still, to find
her way across a room. She takes from them
what she can use, hoping to be amazed.

Mind Leaving

To the mind leaving you, leaving me
—a spent peony bowing down,
dropping petals slowly
on the ground:

I gather your ruby castoffs, float them
in a bowl on my sunroom table,
tell you their descent is
nature's intention.

You continue dancing with breezes
like me. Your mouth still sings,
makes jubilant sounds
as you swirl.

You go on thriving in your roots, draw
sustenance from the past. You
will rise in an altered state.
I'll watch, and hope.

That Sinking Feeling

A drift-log on whitecapped
Lake Michigan, I make
no progress toward a goal
I forget, swallow more
water than I spit out, sink
lower as waves break over
(and over and over).

I ask, will I live longer
than wind and water? No.
Will they wash me up
on shores of afternoon or
night? They might.

I shut my eyes to glaring
light. Peace calls me
from a bench in a park.
I reach out and touch a slat,
which gives me a sliver
of hope I won't founder
on perilous reefs just yet.

Not Giving Up

A new bird is singing.
Maybe it's an old bird
newly wakened.

The song is tentative,
fragmented, like February light,
yesterday's warmth, mist

after a long drought, the whistle
of someone daring to hope
love might restart.

The song trails off,
though the after-song
is surprisingly bright.

I admire life's persistence,
its desire, like the spider's,
not to be crushed, how

ants scramble for cover,
birds retune their voices,
people resist giving up.

Lisa Vihos

Looking for Joy

For so many years,
I've been looking for Joy.

She's always been
ten steps ahead of me.

Clever girl. She was always
on the run, hard to catch.

I followed her footprints
up many mountains and down

to the sea. Never could I keep her
near me. But last night,

in a circle of wise old women,
wrinkled and weary, there she was.

She didn't leave for hours,
as we shared our stories. Maybe,

now that I am becoming old,
Joy will come find me

and sit with me, like she did
when I was a child.

If Joy would give me her attention,
I would ask her, *what kind of house*

would you like? What kind of bed
do you need? I would ask her,

why are you so fleeting, Joy?
What on earth are you looking for?

Fall and Spring

> to an aging man (after Gerard Manley Hopkins)

Yes, Gerard, I am grieving
for the leaves and every leaving,
thoughts that fail, songs unsung.
I feel them slip, though I am young.
Then, as our hearts grow older,
and I feel them burning bolder,
time rushes to deflate me.
But your hungry verse will sate me
and by and by elate me,
as I fall toward you. I flail
and see my ghost set sail.
Your words come close, then flicker far.
Like fireflies, they fill my jar.
I hold them safe and never mourn:
we are, Gerard, in spring reborn.

Vanitas

The Dutch painters got it right,
all those rotting fruits and vegetables
and leaves made lacey by worms.

Candles snuffed out and mirrors cracked.
You see, all material things come to an end
and everything turns yellow with age.

Games grow old and paper, rock, scissors
must end their days. Honey turns crystal,
as things fall apart and leave no trace.

But we remain convinced our legacy lives on
and new birth is waiting for us
just around the corner.

In the Infancy of My Old Age

I am a newbie at this old age thing—
the aches, the pains, the lost keys.
I left a twenty in the money machine
the other morning. Is this how it starts?

Not as old as some, mind you,
not stooped over, I can still
climb a hill, still run a mile. I am
the textbook example of "active senior."

Nearly all the people I work with
could be my children. I throw away
my AARP membership offers, because
I am far too young to retire. But,

slowly, my ankles are giving out
and I greet each new day
with a stiff back, a headache.
Is it my mattress or is it me?

Then, there was that recent scare—severe
chest pain. But it was nothing. I am still
young at heart, though last time I checked,
there were wrinkles in my cleavage.

Reversal

We come into the world
and then go out the same,
incontinent. It isn't supposed to be
like this, is it? I push you in a chair

and bend to tie your shoes.
Those were your jobs.
I used to ask *why this, why that*
and now, that is you asking

and then, not remembering
that I sat with you today.
We know why but we can't
face it, that loss of sharpness,

that inability to maneuver.
Old age visits us now,
an unexpected guest at the table
who came with gifts, yes,

but will not leave until
it has its way with you, with us,
making everything that ever
bothered me about you

multiplied a thousand times,
along with everything
I ever loved.

Marilyn Zelke Windau

Gotcha

Turn on the TV.
Tune in to the 7 p.m. movie on a nondescript channel:
"Saturday Night Fever" is showing with John Travolta
as he used to look before human growth hormone pills and Scientology.
He dances with you in the kitchen while you wash the dinner dishes,
flings an arm out while you mimic with the dish rag.

Then the ads come on.
They capture your attention with funerary desires.
Can you afford to be buried? Can you rely on your children to pay?
Call right now and they will take care of everything.
Your last wishes will be fulfilled at only $19.95 per month
until your last month on earth.

Good tidings will be spoken to whisk you away.
Food and beverages will be provided for the living.
Phone now and the first ten callers will receive
manna from heaven, dealt out in small wafers
from concerned and sympathetic wayfarers.

Back to the movie and the priest brother has resigned.
Parents and Pope cannot figure where they went wrong.
Dancing saves! The rhythm of life drips on at the paint store.
Pizzas prance Bay Ridge avenues.
All seems to come together, especially at the ad break.

Funerals are now discounted to $18.95/month for the next 4 minutes.
They know you do not want to be a burden to your children,
your relatives, your accountant, your minister.
Pick up the phone! You'll be glad you did.
Don't wait until it's too late. Call now!

The next ad is for medication that may cause brain swelling,
diarrhea, shortness of breath, death.
You reach for your phone and dial the 1-800 number
—just to be safe.

Ache Age

There's an old oak.
It's gnarled with deep crevices,
like the ridges in my face.
It pays no mind to those bark-barks.
Leaves and acorns come in due time.
I pay no mind to my wrinkles,
except to placate them with cream.

If you believe in age,
you obtain age.
If you keep young thoughts,
those thoughts keep you young.

Young is a mental state.
It denies chronologic.
It gloms onto Cabbage Patch dolls,
Barbies, Ginnies, Sheras.

Young dreams Mickey Mouse Club,
Bonanza, Dick Clark's American Bandstand,
Walter Cronkite, JFK.

Young dreams Stonehenge, 1066,
1492, 1776, Cinco de Mayo,
your mother's Depression in 1934,
your birth in '49.

You mother-age like your children
mothered teeth—angry, sullen, sore,
yet subdued and placated, then joyful
when the pain of passage eased.

There is an ache-age in its journey.
Prick your finger with a pin.
Compare, analyze, accept the difference.
They both can be moments in time.

Perennial

I refuse to be an annual.
I refuse to give up the ghost
after just one year of growth.
It doesn't matter to me to be seen
as the glory color, the newcomer.

I prefer longevity.
I prefer to come back year after year,
steadfast in my position in the garden of life.
You could call me "Old Faithful"
for I will arise every spring, full of promise,
and I won't disappoint.

You may tire of my need to spread.
You may separate me from my young ones.
I won't be sad.
I know that you will plant my kin forward.
You will find special spots for my progeny.

I will keep you company as you age,
for we all do.
I may toughen my stems or become spindly.
I may get tender skin from sunbaths,
from lack of rain, sparsity of nutrients.
But I will be the plant to count on,
the one you say , "Ah!" to in recognition
year after year.

I will be a perennial.

To Heal or Not Too Heel

Broke.
Broken.
Split.
Chunked.
Strained.
Sprained.
Pulled.
Black. Green. Red. Blue.
Yellow. Olive. Navy.
Puffed.
Ballooned.
Swollen.
Cocktail weenie toes
Slathered with orange sauce.
No weight.
No! Wait!
Six to eight weeks.
Cast.
Outcast.
Weak.
Tired.
Prone.
Crone.
Hell.
Heal.

Threads

As we age, we weave.
We hurl back and forth.
Our footing is not stable.
For those of us of the loom,
it's called tabby, as in cat.
To weavers, it's a strengthening.
It's a normal thrust of shuttle.
It unites threads of color, of texture.
It blends differences of life.

Fibers build unity.
They build design and pattern,
essence of self, of group,
of culture.

Fibers can sing an old song
or a new tune:
the glory of a woolen mill
on the Tay River in Scotland
or a Navaho blanket from Arizona,
error stitched in,
because no human is perfect.

I hug the linen, finely woven,
which was my grandma's.
She kneaded, needed, bread
on that cloth
to gain what is my history.

Acknowledgements

The Grand Avenue Poetry Collective would like the thank the editors of following publications in which these poems first appeared, some in slightly different form:

The Artist's Muse: "Seed Pod"

Fan Mail from Some Flounder (Main Street Rag Publishing, 2018). "Fall and Spring"

Intersections: Art & Poetry (Sheboygan Visual Artists, 2016): "Barn Quilt"

Red Cedar Review: "Hot Flash"

Today I Threw My Watch Away (Finishing Line Press, 2010). "Not Soon, Not Yet"

Wisconsin People and Ideas: "Reversal"

About the poets

Sylvia Cavanaugh

Originally from Pennsylvania, Sylvia Cavanaugh has an M.S. in Urban Planning. She teaches high school African and Asian cultural studies and advises break dancers and poets. A Pushcart Prize nominee, her poems have appeared in various publications. She is a contributing editor for *Verse-Virtual: An Online Community Journal of Poetry*. Her chapbook, *Staring Through My Eyes*, was published by Finishing Line Press in 2016. Her newest chapbook, *Angular Embrace*, by Kelsay Books, was published in 2017. See sylviacavanaugh.com for more.

Nancy Harrison Durdin

Nancy Harrison Durdin enjoyed a career in nursing and now loves writing poetry. She is a member of Wisconsin Fellowship of Poets, Mead Public Library Poetry Circle, as well as The Grand Avenue Poetry Collective. She has been published in WFOP Calendars and Museletters, *Stoneboat Literary Journal*, *An Ariel Anthology* in 2014- 2016, *Brick Street Poetry*, *Words and Other Wild Things*, *Making it Speak: Poets and Artists in Cahoots*, *Intersections/Art and Poetry,* and is a contributing poet for *The Water Poems*, published by Water's Edge Press in 2017.

Dawn Hogue

Dawn Hogue is a Wisconsin writer who lives near Lake Michigan. Her poetry has appeared in *Inscape Magazine, Stoneboat Literary Journal, Making it Speak: Poets & Artists in Cahoots!, Intersections: Art & Poetry,* and *The Wisconsin Fellowship of Poets 2018 Calendar*. She won the Hal Prize for poetry in 2017. Her debut novel, *A Hollow Bone*, is available from Water's Edge Press. Find more at dawnhogue.com.

Maryann Hurtt

Now retired after thirty years of hospice nursing, turning seventy appears to be Maryann Hurtt's next great adventure. Reading, (W)Riting, Running, and Riding (a bright yellow tandem with her husband) remain some of her favorite Rs. She is passionate about clean water and recently completed a manuscript, *Once Upon a Tar Creek: Mining for Voices*. Tar Creek, in northeastern Oklahoma, has been called "the worst environmental disaster no one has heard of." Aldrich Press published *River* in 2016. See maryannhurtt.com for more about her.

Georgia Ressmeyer

Georgia Ressmeyer, an east coast native, has lived in Wisconsin since 1974. Twice nominated for a Pushcart Prize in poetry, in 2017 she received the Honorable Mention Award in the Lorine Niedecker poetry competition sponsored by the Council for Wisconsin Writers. Her most recent full-length poetry collection, *Home/Body*, was published in 2017 by Pebblebrook Press. Other books include an award-winning chapbook, *Today I Threw My Watch Away* (Finishing Line Press, 2010) and a previous full-length collection, *Waiting to Sail* (Black River Press, 2014). She lives near Lake Michigan in Sheboygan. See georgiaressmeyer.com for more information.

Lisa Vihos

Lisa Vihos was born in Chicago and has lived on both coasts, but is happy to have made her home in Sheboygan, Wisconsin since 2002. Her poems have appeared in numerous journals, both print and online. In 2015, she received the first place award in the Wisconsin People and Ideas poetry contest and has two Pushcart Prize nominations. Her fourth chapbook, *Fan Mail from Some Flounder*, was published in 2018 by Main Street Rag Publishing. She is the poetry and arts editor of *Stoneboat Literary Journal*, an occasional guest blogger for *The Best American Poetry* and the Sheboygan organizer for 100 Thousand Poets for Change.

Marilyn Zelke Windau

Marilyn Zelke Windau has never lived far from a lake, particularly, Lake Michigan. A former elementary school art teacher, she enjoys painting with words. Her free verse poems have appeared in many printed and online venues and several anthologies. Her chapbook *Adventures in Paradise* (Finishing Line Press) and a full length, self-illustrated manuscript, *Momentary Ordinary* (Pebblebrook Press) were both published in 2014. *Owning Shadows* (2017) and *Hiccups Haunt Wilson Avenue* (2018) were published by Kelsay Books. She adds her maiden name when she writes to honor her father, who was also a writer.

www.ingramcontent.com/pod-product-compliance
Lightning Source LLC
Chambersburg PA
CBHW030201100526
44592CB00009B/388